Tao Te Ching

A simple, little version of the Tao Te Ching

The Tao of Empty Space

Duane Bruner

Illustrated by Ali Ries (nebula images)
Additional images provided by unsplash.com

Published by Dude Productions

Acknowledgement

The Tao Te Ching is considered the keystone work of the philosophy of Taoism

The founder of Taoism, Lao Tzu, a record-keeper at the Zhou dynasty court, is thought to have lived during the time of Confucius, and his ideas diverged from Confucian beliefs of social classes and rigid rituals. Scholars generally agree that the Tao Te Ching was written by dozens or hundreds of authors over decades or centuries.

Lao Tzu means "Old Master," which has led scholars to question whether or not he ever existed.

Following the Great Proletarian Cultural Revolution in China (1966-1996,) set into motion by Chairman Mao Zedong, Chinese people today have almost no knowledge of the contents of the Tao Te Ching.

In 1981, the Communist Party of China declared that the Cultural Revolution was "responsible for the most severe setback and the heaviest losses suffered by the Party, the country, and the people since the founding of the People's Republic."

In the English language, Tao Te Ching is pronounced "Dao De Jing" or "Dao Duh Jing."

Preface

There are countless translations of the Tao Te Ching, an ancient and classic Chinese text from around the 6th century BC.

The versions I've read have one thing in common—they are difficult to understand. Really difficult. This makes the text inaccessible to a lot of people, and that's a pity because it's a nice piece of work.

I'm trying to bring this classic text to a larger audience with this simplified and modernized version.

I hope I succeed.

If you can't explain it simply,

you don't understand it well enough.

Quote: Albert Einstein and Richard Feynman both made similar statements.

Passage 1

I wish I could, but I can't give you another name for Tao. You might want to call it...way? Or maybe...path?

Knowing Tao is easy, live without desire. Desire prevents you from understanding things as they can be understood. Those who can't do this live with pain and disappointment. It's bound to happen. You see proof all around you.

But naturally you'll have desire. You will also get impatient, mad, sad, angry, jealous and greedy. To hide these feelings increases their force a thousand times. So don't hide them. Use these moments to step outside yourself and examine how these emotions try to control you.

A mind free of thought, merged with itself, touches Tao. Live your life without desire. Live your life without regret.

Come to know Tao.

Passage 2

People see some things as beautiful, and some things as ugly. Some things are seen as good, others are seen as bad.

Some work is seen as easy, while other work is seen as difficult. People also see things as hard or soft, noisy or quiet, high or low.

One with Tao, in harmony with Tao, does not see things this way. He passes no judgment and makes no comparison. He only observes.

One with Tao neither leads nor follows, and what he does is neither big nor small, neither easy or difficult.

He does his work neither slowly nor quickly, and without intent. A task completed deserves no credit, so it can't be discredited. A task completed is a task forgotten.

One with Tao teaches without talking. In this way, his example is never forgotten.

This is a photo of a task forgotten.

Passage 3

One with Tao does not demonstrate skills or wisdom, nor does he praise the talents of others. To do so would create jealousy and rivalry among those who desire wisdom and skill.

Do not seek recognition, status or titles, and others will learn from your example.

Passage 4

Tao is nothing, yet it fills creation endlessly. Tao is hidden, yet it shines everywhere. Tao remains an endless source of nourishment for those in harmony with it. Conduct yourself so as to gain nothing, and awareness of Tao can be achieved and maintained.

Tao files down the sharp edges. Tao loosens the twisted knots. Tao softens the glare and settles the dust. I don't know whose child is Tao. This child was here before the parents.

Passage 5

A master of Tao does not intend to be kind nor benevolent. He has no intentions whatsoever. He is indifferent.

We see examples of this in nature. Nature does not intend to be good when it offers a fine spring day. Nor does it intend to be evil when it brings earthquakes and tsunami. Nature follows Tao.

One with Tao remains tranquil. Neither speech, thought, nor action disturb him.

Passage 6

Tao is empty, yet inexhaustible. Tao is always present within you whether you know it or not.

The meditative mind does not differentiate between right or wrong, good or bad, pleasant or unpleasant. The meditative state is where you will likely first touch Tao.

Tao is infinite and eternal. Eternal because it was never born. Infinite because it has no desires. Tao is present for anyone to absorb.

One with Tao steps behind, therefore, he's always ahead. He's detached from all things and this makes him a part of all things. By letting go of himself he becomes a part of everything.

Passage 8

You can be like water if you want. Managed properly, water helps everything and hurts nothing.

When you hear the sound of flowing water, you almost hear Tao.

Passage 9

For many people, consumption of useless stuff never ends. Who can protect your house when it's full of gold and jade?

The edge of a blade is lost if you sharpen it too much. The more power you have, the more humility you require.

Passage 10

Tao came before the primordial power. Tao is the Mother of the primordial power. Tao is the invisible gateway from which existence came into being.

Without force, Tao guides. Without seeking, Tao serves.

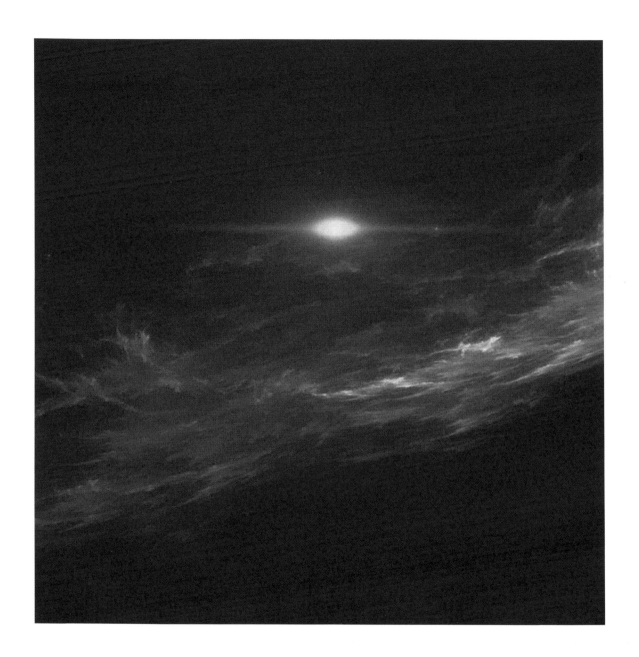

Passage 11

I wish I could, but I can't give you another name for Wu. I need to refer to it, so I call it...empty space.

You can build a house by joining four walls, but only by adding doors and windows, only by adding Wu, empty space, does it become useful.

As with a cup, it is the empty space inside which makes it useful.

Existence alone is dead weight. Only with Wu does it have life. Only with empty space does one with Tao have life.

Passage 12

Sights, sounds and tastes overwhelm the emotions. Galloping about disturbs the mind.

Wasting time acquiring useless stuff impedes growth. Know that an inner truth can be found by losing the senses and stopping useless actions.

Passage 13

Honor and disgrace are two sides of a useless coin. Just throw this coin away.

The Tao which flows through all of us is eternal, therefore we are also eternal. Too many people falsely associate themselves with their bodies. This can result in sorrow, so just throw this idea away, too.

You can slap a master of Tao in the face, but you can't slap him. You can kill the body of a master of Tao, but you can't kill him.

One with Tao knows this truth.

Passage 14

Try to imagine the moment before time began. It's formless, and image-less, but give it a try.

Don't try to see it. In which direction would you look? Don't try to face it. Where would you stand? Don't try to follow it. Where would you go?

Trying to image the moment before time began helps us to understand that what matters is this moment, this moment in time. Knowing the value of this moment brings one closer to Tao.

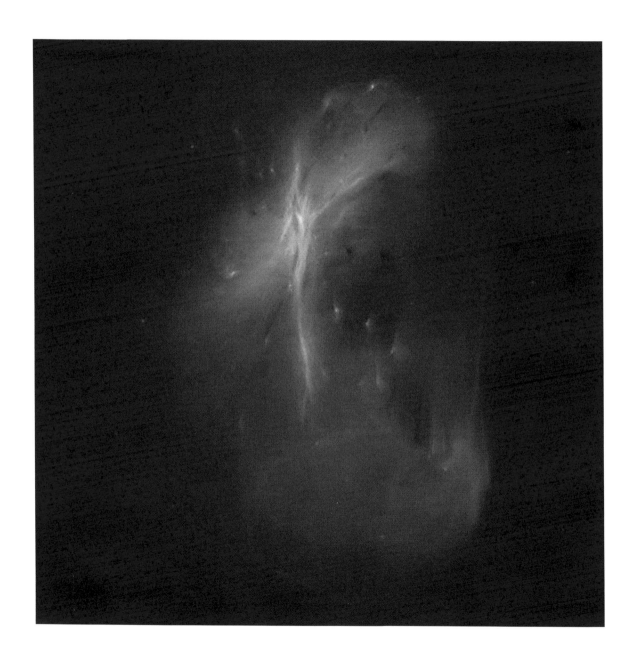

Passage 15

Be deliberate, watchful, mindful, reverent, selfless, dispassionate and pure.

Accept everything like an open valley.

Stop thinking, stop talking, stop doing.

Start breathing, start living, start farming, start baking, start inventing, start engineering, start painting, start sculpting, start writing, start playing.

Stop hurting. Start helping.

Passage 16

When your inner part becomes your outer part, you become indestructible. Become an empty bottle so you can contain everything. You can travel all day without leaving home.

The flourish and the dance, the flashes and the lights, the endless variations of experience and sensation, merge into perfect emptiness when you exit the lion's den.

Passage 17

Great leaders speak little, therefore their words are priceless. Great leaders work without self-interest, and take no credit for their work. When these leaders finish projects, their people say: "This project happened by itself."

Passage 18

Good actions come from the heart of a Taoist. When Tao is absent, actions come from rules like "kindness" or "justice." If one needs rules or laws to be kind and just, something is wrong.

When a family is in disharmony with Tao, we hear them speak of "dutiful sons." When a nation is in chaos, we hear of "loyal ministers" and "great presidents."

Passage 19

Imagine you are only days old, seeing the world for the first time. Do this every moment of every day. It takes training.

Touch everything as if for the first time. Smell every flower, every blade of grass, as if for the first time. Embrace each moment with kindness and simplicity.

Passage 20

I am only a guest in this world. This world is not my real home. While others rush around to get things done, I sit like a fool, aloof and oblivious to the clamor around me.

I appear to be dark and dull. This is not the case. Tao is shining all over me, but it's shining on the inside and no one can see it.

Yes, I'm different. Maybe I'm selfish but I wish there were more people like me.

If you happen to find the Tao Te Ching defeatist, try reading these words again. See if you can see this light. Not everyone gets Tao. That's just the way it is.

Passage 21

Some people ask: "Does Tao actually exist?"

I respond: "Look around you with a silent mind and a selfless heart. If you do this, you might hear the very name that gave me these words. This name is the gate through which the universe entered."

Passage 22

It's strange, but knowing how to follow has put me in command. I never compete, so no one can compete against me.

In my case, surrendering won the war.

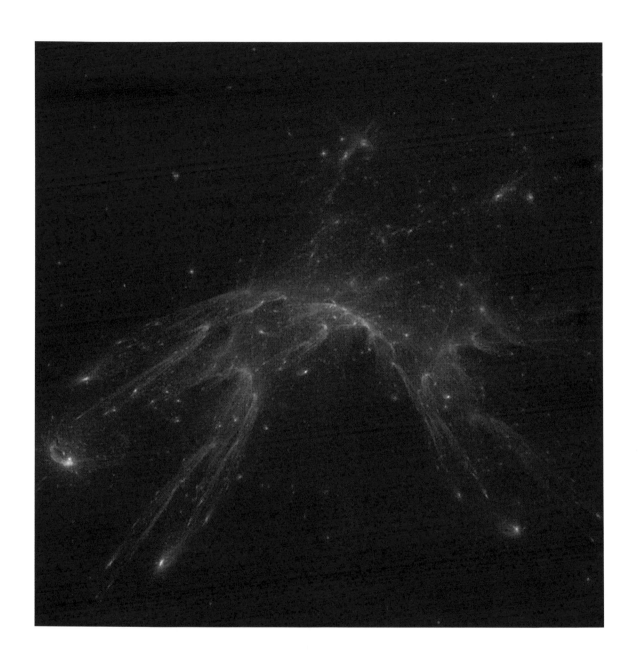

Passage 23

The winds won't blow all day. The rains will stop soon.

When you go from being "the speaker" to "the unspeaking" you will see that it is easier to teach without talking.

Act in accordance with nature and silently follow the flow of the water.

Passage 24

The self-serving never shine, and the self-promoting are always revealed. The self-righteous never endure, and those full of pride die forgotten.

One with Tao never stands on his tiptoes, so he never falls down. He never takes long strides so he never passes anyone.

Passage 25

Tao depends on no one. Tao relies on itself alone. Tao is tranquil and unchanging. Formless, Tao gave form to the universe. Tao makes one supremely free.

Passage 26

Lords of great empires do not go out begging for food. Seeking treasure in this world destroys your roots. Without roots one is restless and weak. Without roots one loses command of many situations.

In the lion's den the views are active, attractive, and they beg attention. One with Tao remains rooted and uninvolved.

Passage 27

I have shut a door in front of me. This door can never be opened. I have also shut the door behind. The door to the left, and to the right. It's like I'm standing in a closet. But this closet has no roof. No floor. And now...no doors.

This place I'm in radiates with Tao. This place is as large as the universe. It's funny, Tao is a great square that has no corners.

Passage 28

There are opposing forces within me. Tao has balanced these forces. I used to swing. Now I'm still. Every breath feels like my first.

Passage 29

Before I knew Tao I was always grasping. Grasping for this, grasping for that.

Trying to change the world always fails. Trying to grasp perfection also fails, but it's worth the effort. The world is a manifestation of Tao, and is therefore perfect.

Suffering people suffer only in their minds. Hunger? That's failure of leadership, and a result of corruption.

Passage 30

If you force a change it will last for a while.
If you gain something from force, you've gained something for a short time only. Force is not in harmony with Tao. Things forced always come to an early end.

Force results in battle and battle curses the land. The land is stripped and the crops fail. Death does no one honor. Battle kills both opponents. One may survive, but he's dead inside. Thoughts of battle need to stop.

Passage 31

It's unfortunate, but sometimes war is the only path to peace. But remember this: when the battle is over, when your enemy is dead, do not celebrate. This battlefield has become sacred ground and you are now at a funeral.

Passage 32

Another strange thing about Tao, it's too easy for people to master.

Some people think too much. Others talk too much. Others do too much. These actions push you away from Tao.

Don't let your life become a trap. Don't let your world become a prison. You are mostly water and this water goes back to the ocean. This water is going back to Tao.

Passage 33

Knowing others is intelligent behavior, knowing yourself is harder. But if you can manage it, the rewards are great.

Approaching life with force, you gain but will not be liked, and no one learns from your example.

Act with force, live long. Act without force, live forever. Conquer yourself and you are immune from any damage.

Passage 34

Taoism is creative quietism, rather than passive contemplation. One with Tao loves the uncertain, he thrives on the mystery. He's made peace with ambiguity. The struggle is over when one touches Tao.

In my view, Taoism is humble philosophy, not religion. Tao makes no claims to greatness. Tao doesn't even know it's great.

Passage 35

Stay silent and let the world pass while holding fast to the form within. Only in this way will this passing world bring you endless joy.

Passage 36

Loss can influence a life. This so-called loss can also give the wisdom of obscurity. Loss can result in a gain. Misfortune can lead to fortune, just as fortune can lead to misfortune.

When you lose a loved one before her time, it creates empty chapters, empty space in your heart and in your mind. This empty space can be of great value. Use it.

Treasure those around you. The young, the old, the mosquitoes, the ants. The monkeys and the dragons.

Passage 37

There is a simplicity of Tao which makes it hard to understand. This simplicity frees the heart from desire. It pushes useless stuff down. This simplicity reveals an inner silence. This simplicity is nameless.

Do nothing though action. Do everything through being. Let the peace and simplicity of Tao shine through.

Passage 38

When Tao is lost, people rely on the rules of virtue. When virtue is lost, people rely on the rules of kindness. When kindness is lost, people rely on the rules of justice. When justice is lost, people rely on the rules of conduct.

When people rely on rules, ignorance abounds. To know Tao, follow your inner nature and listen to your inner voice.

Passage 39

It doesn't matter if you are a gem in a Royal court or a stone on a common path. Live with humility and the glory of Tao will fill you with light.

Passage 40

Tao's way is to yield and to return.

Step aside while others step ahead. Turn your shoulders while others bolt forward. A wise man walks with his head bowed…humble…like the dust.

Passage 41

Now that you've heard of Tao, you might strive with great effort to know it. If so, you are the best seeker of Tao. An average seeker of Tao thinks about Tao now and then.

When the poorest seeker hears of Tao, he laughs out loud, passing judgment on others.

Passage 42

The opposing forces inside me have no name, but I need to refer to them, so I call them "ying" and "yang." Ying gives me support, while yang embraces me.

It is at this still-point, between ying and yang, that I almost touch Tao.

If you grew up without a mother or a father, if you were raised by cousins or strangers, you might feel as if you were never loved. The absence of being loved, while still loving everything, is one way to find this still-point.

This still-point brings you to Tao.

Passage 43

It's hard to find people who keep still, and even harder to find those who keep silent. Taoists are so rare, and that's why so few harvest the beauty of this world.

Passage 44

Sacrifice creates love and generosity creates wealth. Don't be the miser that loses all peace of mind in his pile of money. Owning entangles and wanting bewilders. Avoid the trappings of this world to gain lasting freedom.

Passage 45

Keep walking and you will never get cold. Keep silent and you will never get hot. Be as tranquil as the rains of spring, and as soft as a piece of silk. This is the way, of one, with Tao.

Passage 46

When Tao is present, the horses work the fields. When Tao is absent, war horses spoil sacred ground.

The greatest loss is losing Tao. The greatest curse...desire. Discontentment is the greatest tragedy. Selfishness is the greatest fault.

Passage 47

A master of Tao needs no company. It's not that he dislikes people, he is simply too busy, being not busy, with Tao.

Passage 48

Those who give freely and without attachment gain a full life in return. Those who give with the hope of getting back are merely engaged in business, thus they never receive the treasures of this world.

Passage 49

One with Tao treats good people with goodness. He also treats bad people with goodness. His nature is good, therefore he cannot act any other way.

Treat truthful people with truth. Treat non-truthful people also with truth. Truthfulness is the nature of one with Tao.

A Taoist cannot act any other way, and this draws people toward him. Every eye, every ear, everyone turns toward one with Tao.

Passage 50

Some people follow life and some people follow death. Some people pass from life to death, but they all die in the end by clutching to life in this passing world.

One with Tao is different. Although he walks, he leaves no footprints. Listened for, he cannot be heard. Felt, he cannot be touched. He can walk through walls. No battle, no wild animal, no storm, no earthquake, no fire can harm him.

A man cannot live his life in fear. One with Tao has nothing to fear because he dwells in a place where death cannot enter. He dwells in a place where death does not belong.

Why do I view death so lightly? Because I enjoy life too much to worry. One with Tao knows it is indeed possible to have eternal peace.

Passage 51

I wish I could give you another name for Te, but I can't. While Tao gives life, Te fulfills life. Te is like a magic powder. It raises, it rears, it cultivates and completes. It prepares, comforts and protects.

Honor Tao and Te not with force, but by living and breathing. Create without owning and give without gaining. Do, without claiming.

Passage 52

Stay home, close the mouth, shut the gates and trouble will never find you. Abandon your home, be busy with others and you are beyond rescue.

Insight is knowing that one is small and that strength comes through honoring tenderness. The sun reveals this passing world, and our inner light reveals eternity and brings us back home.

Have faith to follow your own shine. Be aware of your own awareness and you will not stumble, not even on the darkest night.

One with Tao does not smile on the brightest days, nor does he frown on the darkest. This does not mean he is incapable of happiness or sadness. It simply means that he is lost within the endless energy of Tao.

When you meet such a person, perhaps now you will understand him.

Passage 53

Knowing Tao takes no wisdom at all. The path is easy to find. It is simple, direct, clear of every rock and pebble, every piece of sand. But people love to detour to paths strewn with rocks, pebbles and sand. Therefore, they stumble.

Have you seen how magnificent the people have become? With their colorful gowns and colorful gems? Their expensive watches, phones and cars?

Food and drink overflow. Wealth and soft living abound, yet in some places the fields are barren, the granaries empty, and people are forced to go on the run.

Pomp at the expense of others…one with Tao cannot understand this.

Passage 54

Tao is everywhere. To see it in a person, see it as a person. To see it in a family, see it as a family. To see it in a country, see it as a country. To see it in the world, see it as a world.

A person embodied with Tao is true. A family embodied with Tao thrives. A country embodied with Tao prospers. A world embodied with Tao is perfection. A universe embodied with Tao gives birth to a new universe.

Passage 55

One with Tao is oblivious to the union of male and female, yet his vitality is full, his inner spirit complete. But one in harmony with Tao never looks down on anyone, nor does he look up.

He understands that the union of male and female ensures the survival of the species, and sometimes creates new Taoists.

Passage 56

There is indeed a secret quality embracing one with Tao. The knots loosen when one becomes the dust of the world. The glare tempers. The insights gain. The passions pass.

Be beyond the cares of men to become the dearest place in their hearts.

Passage 57

Rulers of state have a plan. These plans rarely work. More restrictions lead to more poverty. More weapons lead to more fear. More cleverness leads to less cleverness. More laws lead to more lawbreakers.

Lift up those around you by loving your own life. Try it, it works.

Those who join battles, I don't understand them.

Give without conditions and everyone prospers. Want nothing to have everything.

Passage 58

Illusion and delusion abound. This will always be the case. Tao guides you back. Tao cuts but does not harm. Tao straightens without disrupting. Tao illumines without dazzling.

Find Tao now and there will be nothing you cannot overcome. There will be no obstacles, no limits, no empire you cannot rule.

Tao runs so thick in the blood. Like a huge tree, Tao gives you deep roots and a solid trunk.

Passage 60

There are dark and harmful people out there. When a master of Tao approaches, these cowards rush in to sweep his path.

Passage 61

Be like a river basin and accept everything flowing through your life. A river basin is where all things come to rest, and where all things are welcome.

When a master of Tao bows to you, and when you bow back and raise your head, both the Master, and you, see only respect.

Passage 62

Do not cast wicked people away, it's better to awaken them with your actions. Elevate them with your deeds. Heal their injuries with softness and kindness.

You can cast away their wickedness but you cannot cast them away.

Passage 63

Sometimes injury leads one to Tao. Tao leads one to blessings.

Life doesn't have to be so hard. Seeing difficulties as opportunities leads to no difficulties at all.

Passage 64

A mind at peace makes difficulties easy to overcome.

Finish a task before it becomes hard. Put things in order before they get out of hand. Be patient and your work will never fail. Be steady at the beginning to win the race.

Passage 65

Rulers with clever ideas fill people's lives with hardship. In ancient times this was not the case. Rulers blended with the common people.

Te seeks Tao and this movement guides the universe. This movement guides us back home in a way rulers and their rules can never do.

Passage 66

The seas stay below everything, and this is why rivers rush towards them.

If you wish to help people, speak below them. If you wish to lead people, walk behind them. Remain a servant to become a king.

Three treasures to hold dear. Love. Moderation. Humility.

Tao does not protect with an army. It protects with these three treasures.

Passage 68

This path I speak of leads to perfection. It leads without haste. It leads without waste.

It wins fights without fighting. It overcomes without confronting.

Passage 69

The greatest warriors prefer to be guests, not hosts. They prefer to retreat a foot instead of gaining an inch.

You can advance without your feet. You can seize without your arms. You can teach without a sword. You can fight without using a muscle.

The phrase "I have an enemy" is the saddest phrase of all. When "I" and "enemy" exist together, Tao is lost.

When two opponents meet, the one without an enemy is going to win.

Passage 70

Those who understand Tao are rare. Those who follow Tao, even rarer. Look for them. Find them. Learn from them. They will be hard to find as they do not display their skills.

They can wear the clothes of a beggar and still contain a gem within.

This is a photo of a Master of Tao.

Passage 71

Trying to understand what cannot be fully understood is a worthwhile goal. A great tragedy is not knowing what needs to be known.

Know how little you know—be well. Know how much you know—be ill.

One with Tao is free, and everyplace is the perfect place to be.

Every place is home.

Passage 72

View yourself without limits. If the conditions of your birth were not the best, don't despise.

One with Tao knows himself, but not as himself. One with Tao loves himself, but not as himself. One with Tao honors himself, but not as himself. In this way, he loses himself and gains all that can be gained.

Passage 73

Who can know the source of creation? Who can know this endless universe?

One with Tao bothers not with these questions, but he does not look down on those who do.

Passage 74

Death threats are useless against those who have no fear of death. If death is the fate handed to lawbreakers, who would dare do the killing?

All life, from the highest to the lowest, is precious, and none can ever be replaced.

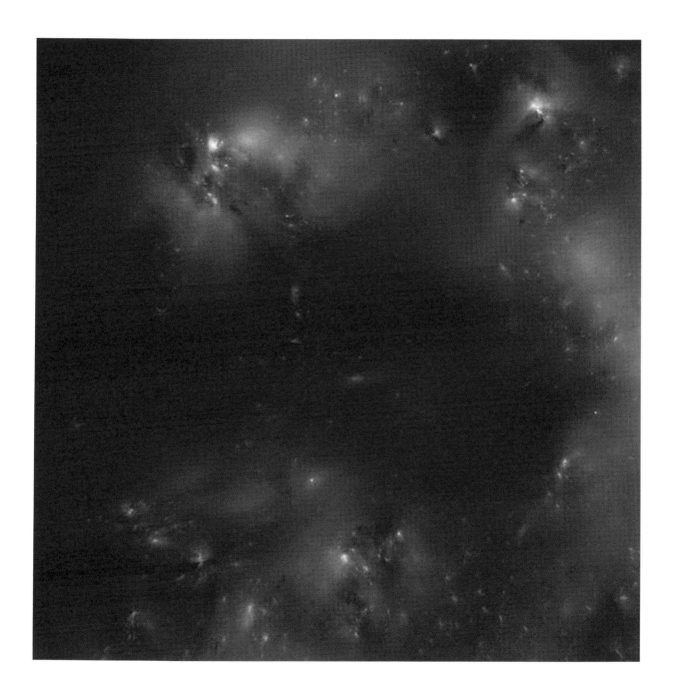

Passage 75

People starve when the grain is consumed by corruption. People rebel when those in power meddle with their lives.

Hold on to things and miss the treasures of this world. Treasure is gained by letting go.

Passage 76

As babies we are tender and weak, as seniors, brittle and dry. All things, even grass and trees, are soft and pliable when young, dry and brittle in death.

An army that never yields will always fail. A tree that won't bend cracks in the wind. By natures own decree, the hard and strong are defeated, the gentle and weak triumph.

Passage 77

One with Tao bends like a bow. The high and mighty are pulled down while the humble rise.

Too many take from those who have nothing, only to give to those who have everything. One with Tao gives without even trying. He does his job without looking for reward. One with Tao shines without stepping from the shadows.

Passage 78

Although water is soft and yielding, nothing is better at wearing down the hard and strong. Water is weak, but it can't be hurt. Water is soft, but it can't be damaged. Water yields, but never wears away.

Softness overcomes hardness. Yielding overcomes rigidity. These are things everyone knows.

So why do so few practice this?

Passage 79

Resentment often remains when a great dispute is settled. Avoid disputes by being happy with what you have.

Seek ways to give, and virtue is gained. Seek ways to gain, and virtue is lost.

Tao plays no favorites but naturally sides with the pure heart.

Passage 80

Live in a small village with few people and walk where you need to go.

There will be tools to speed things up, 10 times or 10,000 times, yet no one will use them. There will be cars, boats, trains and airplanes, but there will be no passengers.

Let the weapons and armor collect dust.

Who walks into a forest and accuses the trees of being off-center? Who walks to the shore and tell the waves they are imperfect?

Virtue is gained by not looking for faults in others. One loses virtue when looking for faults.

Those who come to know Tao do not learn it. Those who try to learn it have trouble understanding it.

Close the mouth. Close the mind. Open the heart. Touch Tao.

All things go as Tao goes. All things flow like water.

Afterword

This simple, little version of the Tao Te Ching makes for a unique and affordable birthday or holiday gift. See us on Amazon and at emptyspacemovie.com.
All proceeds from the sale of Duane's books help to fund the science-fiction journey:

Empty Space

Episode One
"Stone Knives and Bearskins"

And coming to Amazon 2016
Empty Space Just Got Bigger (*a free eBook*)

by
Duane Bruner

If you would like your photo to be part of this next book, please submit photo(s) for consideration by March 15, 2016 at www.emptyspacemovie.com

See more at:

www.emptyspacemovie.com
On Facebook: Dude Productions

On Kickstarter: May 1, 2016 (Empty Space)

From the author

I graduated from the University of Missouri - Columbia in 1986 with a BA in Journalism.

From 1986 - 2008, I worked for Grey Worldwide, an advertising agency, in New York, Dusseldorf, Zurich, Madrid, Lisbon, Belgium, London, Mexico City, Shanghai, Hong Kong, Manila and Bangkok.

In 2012 I created the entertainment project "Command Magellan," a one-hour TV science fiction drama, and wrote the first version of the script. It just didn't work.

In 2015 I created the entertainment project "Empty Space" and wrote the first version of the script. It works better.

This book, The Tao of Empty Space, was started in 2007 and completed in 2015. I'd like to thank Oliver Benjamin, the founder of Dudeism, for forcing me to complete this work. (Note to Oliver: Bastard, you gave me a heart attack! ;)

In 2015 Duane founded Dude Productions in Chiang Mai, Thailand. We're closing our doors in 2018 and going bowling.

Printed in Great Britain
by Amazon